LET'S EXPLORE BRITAIN

Forests

JAMES NIXON

Raintree is an imprint of Capstone Global Library Limited, a company incorporated in England and Wales having its registered office at 264 Banbury Road, Oxford, OX2 7DY – Registered company number: 6695582

www.raintree.co.uk
myorders@raintree.co.uk

Edited by James Nixon
Designed by Keith Williams, sprout.uk.com
Picture Research by James Nixon
Production by Discovery Books
Originated by Capstone Global Library Limited
Printed and bound in India

ISBN 978 1 4747 5898 7 (hardback)
22 21 20 19 18
10 9 8 7 6 5 4 3 2 1

ISBN 978 1 4747 5902 1 (paperback)
23 22 21 20 19
10 9 8 7 6 5 4 3 2 1

Northamptonshire Libraries & Information Services KK	
Askews & Holts	

Acknowledgements
We would like to thank the following for permission to reproduce photographs:
Cover image (Mcimage/Shutterstock); Alamy: pp. 8 (Scottish Viewpoint), 21 (Carpe Diem), 23 (Chris Strickland), 24 (South West Images Scotland), 25 (Arterra Picture Library), 28 (Mint Photography), 29 (Veryan Dale); Shutterstock: pp. 4 (stocker1970), 5 (Nataliia Politova), 6 (David Young), 7 (Phillip Maguire), 9 (Dave Head), 10 (Helen Hotson), 11 (AlineBehrendt Photography), 12 and 13 (PJ photography), 14 (Mark Caunt), 15 (Ondrej Prosicky), 16 (Zadiraka Evgenii), 17 (Kristian Bell), 18 (Simon Bratt), 19 (Martin Fowler), 20 (Erni), 22 (ImagesbyInfinity), 26 (Sally Wallis), 27 (sw_photo).

We would like to thank Dr Gillian Fyfe for her invaluable help in the preparation of this book.

Contents

What are forests?

Forests are large areas of land covered by trees. Every forest has its own character. Trees come in many shapes and sizes. They provide food and homes for different types of wildlife. Forests can be found in nearly all parts of Britain. Do you know the name of the forest closest to where you live?

In Britain, woodland covers about 13 per cent of the land.

Trees start as small seeds which grow into **seedlings**. The seeds can fall from trees nearby and grow naturally. Or they may be planted by people. Forests can take decades or centuries to develop. When the trees grow tall, they block out the light. This stops smaller trees and **shrubs** from growing.

This young forest still has a layer of shrubs covering the ground.

Types of woodland

There are two main types of woodland. **Deciduous** forests contain trees with flat, green leaves. Their leaves die in autumn and usually fall to the forest floor. On the ground, the leaves build up into a layer called **leaf litter**. Oak, beech, silver birch and types of chestnut are deciduous trees.

Epping Forest is a deciduous woodland on the edge of London.

Coniferous forests contain evergreen trees. Evergreen trees have tough, hardy leaves that can survive the winter. Their leaves are often shaped like needles. Trees such as pines and spruces can grow very high. They make cones to produce seeds.

There are many large coniferous forests in the Scottish Highlands.

Queen Elizabeth Forest Park

Britain's biggest forests

Britain's biggest forest is the Galloway Forest Park in southern Scotland. It covers a massive area measuring 777 square kilometres (300 square miles). The forest is so large and **remote** that it makes night times very dark. In 2009, the forest became Britain's first **Dark Sky Park**.

Dark Sky Parks such as Galloway Forest are fantastic places to watch the stars and planets.

Kielder Forest in Northumberland is England's largest forest. In total, it measures 650 square kilometres (250 square miles). The forest was planted in the 1920s to supply Britain with wood. Both Galloway and Kielder forests are planted mainly with sitka spruce. Sitka spruce grows very well in wet, hilly areas.

Kielder Forest surrounds Kielder Water.
It is the biggest human-made lake in the UK.

Changing forests

Ancient woodlands are woods and forests that are at least 400 years old. Many forests have been there for thousands of years. These woods grew naturally and contain lots of **native** trees. The mix of trees and the old, dead wood make these brilliant **habitats** for wildlife. Just two per cent of British land is now ancient woodland.

The ancient oaks in Wistman's Wood, Devon, are all twisted and covered in moss.

A lot of ancient woodland has been cut down and replaced with conifers. These are planted to produce **timber**. Huge conifer **plantations** are often packed tightly with just one or two types of trees. Trees are chosen that grow fast and straight. These types of forests contain much less wildlife than native forests.

Douglas firs, like these, are the tallest trees in Britain.

As the seasons go by, trees **react** to the changing weather. When it gets too cold, **deciduous** trees shut down for the winter. Before their leaves fall, they change colour. They turn from green, to orange, red or yellow. Finally the leaves go brown and shrivel. Some conifers drop their needles, too.

A family takes an autumn walk through Standish Wood in Gloucestershire.

In spring, the temperature rises. The trees wake up and start to produce a new set of leaves. The leaves emerge from **buds** and uncurl themselves. In the summer, the trees' leaves get darker and tougher. This helps protect them from leaf-eating bugs.

In spring, Standish Wood bursts into life.

Animals in the forest

Forests are full of life from top to bottom. The highest part of the forest is called the **canopy**. Large birds of prey, such as buzzards, live up among the branches. They make nests from twigs and small branches. Other birds feed in the tree tops. Crossbills use their special beaks to pick seeds out from under the cones' scales.

The crossbill has an unusual bill. The top and bottom of the bill crosses over at its tip.

Lower down on the tree trunks, birds such as woodpeckers and treecreepers peck at the bark. They hunt for flies, spiders and other insects to eat. Many thousands of minibeasts live in the **leaf litter** on the ground. Beetles, worms and woodlice feed on the rotting leaves and wood.

The male stag beetle has **pincers** that look like a deer's **antlers**.

Many types of animal depend on woodland for their survival. Owls, squirrels and some types of bats nest in the holes of trees. The red squirrel is one of Britain's most famous woodland creatures. It is now rare and **under threat**. Grey squirrels are bigger and stronger. They have taken over many of the red squirrels' old **habitats**.

Red squirrels search for nuts, seeds and berries to eat.

Hungry deer strip the leaves and **buds** off trees and **shrubs**. The red deer is Britain's biggest land animal. Badgers are strong diggers that tunnel underground in woodland. They build large burrows called setts. The wild boar died out around 700 years ago, but is now back in some British forests.

A wild boar family with piglets roam the Forest of Dean in Gloucestershire.

Plants and fungi

Before the trees grow new leaves in spring, wild flowers bloom on the forest floor. You may see yellow primroses, white wood anemones or a carpet of bluebells. In summer, thorny **shrubs** such as wild roses and blackberries grow. In conifer forests, **ferns** and mosses grow in the damp, shady conditions.

Millions of bluebells can grow closely together. They make spectacular displays.

A wonderful variety of **fungi** can be found in forests. Fungi feed on tree roots, dead wood and other rotten material in the **leaf litter**. They have threads that branch out through the soil and wood. We can see fungi when they grow into mushrooms or toadstools.

Honey fungus can grow large numbers of mushrooms on tree stumps and rotting wood.

WARNING: Some fungi are poisonous. Never touch one without an adult's permission.

Protecting the forests

Humans have been cutting down forests for thousands of years. Trees are cut for **timber**. They are also cleared to make space for farmland and buildings. Since the 1930s, more than half of Britain's ancient woodland has been destroyed. The future of many plants and animals is in danger.

The tiny dormouse is losing many of its woodland **habitats**. It needs protection.

The Woodland Trust works to save forests and creatures that are **under threat**. The Trust owns and protects over 1,000 pieces of forest in Britain. Many of these forests are ancient. The Trust's work helps animals such as the dormouse. New forests are also planted to create spaces for wildlife.

The Woodland Trust has planted over half a million trees in Heartwood Forest in Hertfordshire. This has made it the largest forest with **native** trees in England.

Using forests

Centuries ago, some forests were used as hunting grounds. They were called royal forests. People hunted mainly deer, but also wild boar and wolves. The New Forest was turned into a royal forest in 1079 by the King of England. Sherwood Forest in Nottinghamshire was another royal forest. In legend, this was the home of Robin Hood.

Ponies have grazed in the New Forest, Hampshire, for thousands of years.

Today, the Forestry Commission owns 20 per cent of our forests. The Commission was set up in the 1920s to solve Britain's shortage of **timber**. Workers are also helping to turn forests into places that people can visit and enjoy. Looking after wildlife is important, too.

A forest worker checks on the chicks in an osprey's nest. An osprey is a large bird of prey.

Timber is valuable and has many uses. The wood is used to construct buildings, furniture and fences. It can also be **pulped** and turned into paper. There are many jobs for people in the timber industry. Forest workers called **loggers** use heavy machinery to cut down the trees.

Machines called harvesters fell trees with a chainsaw on the end of a long arm. The logger sits in the cab for safety.

Loggers also operate vehicles called forwarders. Forwarders lift cut trees out of the forests. The logs are piled up into stacks and then loaded onto a lorry. **Plantations** must be managed carefully. Foresters choose which trees to plant and look after **seedlings**. They must also guard against the spread of fires and diseases in trees.

Forwarders have a trailer on the back for transporting logs.

Forest fun

Forestry Commission tracks are free to use for walkers, cyclists and horse riders. Forests are popular because they are beautiful and peaceful. They give visitors a chance to explore and exercise at the same time. Some people visit forests to track down rare wildlife, such as the red squirrel.

Horse riders can ride through forests on tracks called bridleways.

Forest trails have been specially built for walkers and mountain bikers. Mountain bike trails are thrilling. They twist and turn and are full of bumps. The toughest tracks contain downhill jumps. At **trail centres**, riders can attempt a number of different routes.

The first ever trail centre for mountain bikers was opened in Coed-y-Brenin Forest in North Wales.

Forestry Commission forests have 70 million visitors every year. Lots of forests have cafés and adventure playgrounds. Holiday villages have been built in some forests. There are plenty of activities to do there. Children can enjoy birdwatching, building dens or following nature trails.

This holiday village opened in Woburn Forest, Bedfordshire, in 2014.

Some companies run tree-top adventure courses in forests across Britain. The daring courses have wobbly rope bridges and cargo nets. They also have tunnels, swings and zip wires. Safety lines are attached to people to stop them from falling.

A girl attempts an adventure course in Dalby Forest, North Yorkshire.

Map of the UK

Here are the locations
of the forests mentioned
in this book.

Queen Elizabeth Forest Park

Galloway Forest Park

Kielder Forest

Dalby Forest

Sherwood Forest

Coed-y-Brenin Forest

Woburn Forest

Heartwood Forest

Epping Forest

Forest of Dean

Standish Wood

Wistman's Wood

New Forest

Glossary

antlers horns on the head of an adult deer

bud bulge on a plant's stem that develops into a leaf or flower

canopy highest branches on the trees in a forest

coniferous coniferous trees produce cones and have green leaves or needles all year round

Dark Sky Parks protected places in the world for watching stars in the night sky

deciduous deciduous trees drop their leaves every year

ferns plants that have leaves shaped like feathers but do not produce flowers

fungi mushrooms, toadstools and moulds which feed on rotting material

habitat place where a plant or animal lives

leaf litter rotting leaves and other material that forms a layer on top of the soil

loggers workers who cut down trees for timber

native native trees grew naturally in a specific country or area, and were not introduced by humans

pincers front claws of an insect

plantation large area in which trees have been planted for timber

pulped mashed up into a soft, wet material

react respond to something in a certain way

remote far away from towns and cities

seedling very young plant or tree

shrub woody plant that is much smaller than a tree

timber wood used as a building material

trail centre place where trails have been built specially for mountain bikers

under threat in danger of dying out

Find out more

Books

I Love This Tree: Discover the Life, Beauty and Importance of Trees, Anna Claybourne (Franklin Watts, 2016)

Woodland and Forest, Jamie Ambrose (Dorling Kindersley, 2017)

Woodland (Fact Cat), Izzi Howell (Wayland, 2016)

Websites

www.forestry.gov.uk/visit
Forestry Commission: *Find your local forest and discover what activities you can do.*

www.woodlandtrust. org.uk/visiting-woods/ trees-woods-and-wildlife
Woodland Trust: *Learn everything you need to know about Britain's trees and woodland wildlife.*

Index